Titles by Langaa R

Francis B. Nyamnjoh
Stories from Abakwa
Mind Searching
The Disillusioned African
The Convert
Souls Forgotten
Married But Available

Dibussi Tande
No Turning Back. Poems of Freedom 1990-1993

Kangsen Feka Wakai
Fragmented Melodies

Ntemfac Ofege
Namondo. Child of the Water Spirits
Hot Water for the Famous Seven

Emmanuel Fru Doh
Not Yet Damascus
The Fire Within
Africa's Political Wastelands: The Bastardization of
Cameroon
Oriki'badan
Wading the Tide

Thomas Jing
Tale of an African Woman

Peter Wuteh Vakunta
Grassfields Stories from Cameroon
Green Rape: Poetry for the Environment
Majunga Tok: Poems in Pidgin English
Cry, My Beloved Africa
No Love Lost
Straddling The Mungo: A Book of Poems in English &
French

Ba'bila Mutia
Coils of Mortal Flesh

Kehbuma Langmia
Titabet and the Takumbeng

Victor Elame Musinga
The Barn
The Tragedy of Mr. No Balance

Ngessimo Mathe Mutaka
Building Capacity: Using TEFL and African Languages as
Development-oriented Literacy Tools

Milton Krieger
Cameroon's Social Democratic Front: Its History and
Prospects as an Opposition Political Party, 1990-2011

Sammy Oke Akombi
The Raped Amulet
The Woman Who Ate Python
Beware the Drives: Book of Verse

Susan Nkwentie Nde
Precipice

**Francis B. Nyamnjoh &
Richard Fonteh Akum**
The Cameroon GCE Crisis: A Test of Anglophone
Solidarity

Joyce Ashuntantang & Dibussi Tande
Their Champagne Party Will End! Poems in Honor of
Bate Besong

Emmanuel Achu
Disturbing the Peace

Rosemary Ekosso
The House of Falling Women

Peterkins Manyong
God the Politician

George Ngwane
The Power in the Writer: Collected Essays on Culture,
Democracy & Development in Africa

John Percival
The 1961 Cameroon Plebiscite: Choice or Betrayal

Albert Azeyeh
Réussite scolaire, faillite sociale : généalogie mentale de
la crise de l'Afrique noire francophone

Aloysius Ajab Amin & Jean-Luc Dubois
Croissance et développement au Cameroun :
d'une croissance équilibrée à un développement équitable

Carlson Anyangwe
Imperialistic Politics in Cameroun:
Resistance & the Inception of the Restoration of the
Statehood of Southern Cameroons

Bill F. Ndi
K'Cracy, Trees in the Storm and Other Poems

**Kathryn Toure, Therese Mungah
Shalo Tchombe & Thierry Karsenti**
ICT and Changing Mindsets in Education

Charles Alobwed'Epie
The Day God Blinked

G.D. Nyamndi
Babi Yar Symphony
Whether losing, Whether winning
Tussles: Collected Plays

Samuel Ebelle Kingue
Si Dieu était tout un chacun de nous?

Ignasio Malizani Jimu
Urban Appropriation and Transformation : bicycle, taxi
and handcart operators in Mzuzu, Malawi

Justice Nyo' Wakai:
Under the Broken Scale of Justice: The Law and My
Times

John Eyong Mengot
A Pact of Ages

Ignasio Malizani Jimu
Urban Appropriation and Transformation: Bicycle Taxi
and Handcart Operators

Joyce B. Ashuntantang
Landscaping and Coloniality: The Dissemination of
Cameroon Anglophone Literature

Jude Fokwang
Mediating Legitimacy: Chieftaincy and Democratisation in
Two African Chiefdoms

Michael A. Yanou
Dispossession and Access to Land in South Africa: an
African Perspecvtive

Tikum Mbah Azonga
Cup Man and Other Stories

John Nkemngong Nkengasong
Letters to Marions (And the Coming Generations)

Wading the Tide

Poems by
Emmanuel Fru Doh

Langaa Research & Publishing CIG
Mankon, Bamenda

Publisher:
Langaa RPCIG
(*Langaa* Research & Publishing Common Initiative Group)
P.O. Box 902 Mankon
Bamenda
North West Province
Cameroon
Langaagrp@gmail.com
www.langaapublisher.com

Distributed outside N. America by African Books Collective
orders@africanbookscollective.com
www.africanbookscollective.com

Distributed in N. America by Michigan State University
Press
msupress@msu.edu
www.msupress.msu.edu

ISBN: 9956-558-77-X

DISCLAIMER

This is a work of fiction. Names, characters, places, and incidents are either the author's invention or they are used fictitiously. Any resemblance to actual places and persons, living or dead, events, or locales is coincidental.

Dedication

For my father,

PHILIP DOH AWAH

and my mother

THERESIA LUM

for all they have been to us,

and for

The oppressed minority
of this once beautiful country,
that as we struggle for
freedom and our integrity,
our sacrifice and the blood of
all those who have died in the struggle
may not go in vain.

Contents

Preface vii
Introduction ix

UPRISING
Down Time-Avenue 3
The Seasons 4
Kwashiorkor Graveyard 5
Njangi House 5
Quite a Deal 6
Land of Prawns 7
The Bloody Caps 8
This is my Chop-Chair 9
The Politician Never Learns 9
Lament of the Town-Crier 10
Bamenda *Chop Fire* 11
Life on Campus 13
Shame Africa 14
Negritude At Dusk 15
The Black Queen 16
Who Do They Think They Are Fooling 17

TRIBUTE
The *Maquisards* ··· 21
The Poet-Soldier ··· 22
The Light That Never Shone ································· 23
Just After Nine Rains ·· 24
To A Queen At Dusk ··· 25
Kamah ·· 26
And They Killed Che-Ngwa Ghandi ···················· 26
The Quest ·· 28
The Amazon ·· 29

Bamenda 29
Where I Do Not Belong 30

NOSTALGIA
Meeting After So Long 35
Parting Ways 36
Gone With The Seventies 37
This Maze 38
The Abyss Of The Past 38
Dilemma Children 39
Rain Clouds 40

THE OUTCAST
The Taste of Foam 43
Samson And Delilah 43
Fear The White Man's Country 44

Preface

Wading the Tide was first published in1995 by Patron Publishing House, Bamenda, Cameroon, and later in 1998 by Kola Tree Press in Bellingham, WA, U.S.A. Accordingly, this Langaa edition which comes fourteen years after the first edition, is timely because of the need to continue circulating a volume of poems that won the hearts of many—scholars and lay members of society alike—especially in Cameroon, the geographical setting and main thematic concern of a good number of the poems in the volume. It is possibly the political era the volume covers, especially in the section "Uprising", that brought about its popularity. Indeed, many of the poems touch on a historically turbulent political era in Cameroon's history when the proletariat stood up against the existing regime and its clinging to power through the rigging of elections. The relevance and great value of this newest edition, therefore, cannot be overemphasized as the status quo in Cameroon is no different from what it was almost two decades ago; if nothing else, it has deteriorated further instead.

From many different perspectives, the people of Cameroon, and Africa in general, can especially relate to the political themes treated in the first section "Uprising," and to the rest of the poems, of course. This is the case because beyond politics and the unfortunate socio-economic predicament of Cameroon, in particular, and Africa at large, *Wading the Tide* is a volume about humankind and his environment as it treats love, pain, death, and so much more, while also paying tribute to different, deserving personages. This is a volume that conscientizes by highlighting a struggling nation and continent's predicament in a modern world order that cares less about the suffering who have been conveniently categorized and labeled as the Third World. Yet this Third World, especially Africa, is indeed not as poor as they would love one to believe; this is a continent that, because of its overwhelming material wealth and rich labour force, has been blatantly exploited by the existing world order for the wellbeing of subjects of the so-called First World or industrialized nations, thanks to the machinations of the first world and its monetary organizations. This is a volume then that reveals the true nature and in some ways, the *raison d'être* of Africa's backwater situation with the hope of opening the eyes of the continent's exploited to their plight in anticipation that someday they will understand why one part of the world continues to flourish while the other stagnates. In the case of Cameroon, it is hoped the exploited lot will understand why citizens of some parts of the country were ready to die in the process of storming the corrupt and irresponsible Etoudi machinery manifesting its treacherous grip over the nation while others went on with life as if nothing was happening.

The socio-political atmosphere in Cameroon, in particular, and Africa, as a whole, that holds sway over much of this volume is yet to change; in fact, it has deteriorated further even as Cameroon today, in particular, seems to be a nation without a leader. Besides the incumbent's characteristically tasteless and uninspiring speeches to the citizens on the eve of every new year, not only does the president not seem to have a plan for Cameroon's ailing economy and the prevailing state of anomy which is so bad one cannot talk of a "system" in place, he does not really seem to care. Apparently, his only feasible plan, like many other African Quixotes masquerading as heads of states, is to die in office; what a socio-economic investment to bequeath the citizenry of a nation that was once a bastion of integrity and peace not that long ago. And so under a lackadaisical regime, the Cameroonian nation continuous to sink into near nonsense with her citizens now learning quickly to survive by hook or by crook, a policy that was never Cameroonian, but which today has distinguished the nation as one of the most corrupt in the world.

One can only hope that as Cameroonians, and Africans in general, continue to read these poems, they may learn, besides much else, about the bad hand they have been dealt, especially by local yet unrepresentative governments that continue to maintain themselves in office, very often with the support of hypocritical alien powers, even though they are without plans for improving upon the exploited and impoverished lot of their nations—the Third World.

Emmanuel Fru Doh
Minnesota,
February, 2009.

Introduction

This introduction would not have been necessary were it not for the fact that critics of African literature tend to compartmentalize the new poet in a manner that deprives him of his individuality, his uniqueness. The poem is not an event in social history nor a symptom of a literary movement, it is an assertion of the poet's singular identity.

Art, Tolstoy tells us, is a human activity consisting in the fact that one man consciously, by means of certain external signs, hands on to others feeling he has lived through, and that others are infected by those feelings and also experience them. Something in the heart of each of us vibrates to the joys and sorrows of others.

The poet is first and foremost an individual with a personal vision. This "Introduction", I must warn at once, is not a key to the unravelling of the mysteries which may lurk behind Doh's poetic expression. Every good reader responds to good poetry, each in his own manner.

Records will show that Anglophone Cameroon has produced many more poets than short story writers, dramatists and novelists. Hardly a month passes without a poem featuring in one or more of the popular newspapers! What has not been generally done on a serious scale, and what we find tremendously innovative here, is the bringing together of those splinters of poetic visitations into the sort of challenging web of poetic composition we are beholding here. The accomplishment is not numerical but intrinsic. The poems are weighty, touching, enduring.

Some will remonstrate, and with good reason, that Doh cannot be said to have said what has never been said before! For instance, an avid reader of African poetry from the thirties can quite easily discover analogues and antecedents: Doh's "The Seasons" (from UPRISING) remind one of Kwesi Brew's "The Dry Season," and Wole Soyinka's "Season"; "Shame Africa" (from UPRISING) reminds us of Grail Armattoe's "Africa," Dei Anang's "Dear Africa," and David Diop's "Africa"; "The Light that Went Out" (from TRIBUTE) recalls to mind Lenrie Peter's "The Fire Has Gone Out", "Lament of the Town-Crier" (from TRIBUTE) reminds one of Fale Wache's "Lament of a Mother", and Okogbule Wonodi's "Lament for 'Shola"; "Bamenda" (from TRIBUTE) reminds us of" J.P. Clark's "Ibadan"; "Parting Ways" (from NOSTALGIA) reminds us of Christopher Okigbo's "Love Apart.."

What this means is that Doh is thinking about his subject, just as other poets before him did. Like any other poet, he is extremely sensitive and acutely aware of the world in which he lives, the human predicament, the beauty of the weather, the horrors of war and dirty politics, the love of one person for another, the angers, sorrows, pleasures of everyday living. In her very important chapter "Poetry and the Human Predicament," (in *Poetry: A Modern Guide to Its Understanding and Enjoyment*) Elizabeth Drew listed seven aspects through which poetry manifests the human predicament: Time, Death, Frustration and Loneliness, Social Satire, Nature, Love, Humanism and Religion. *Wading the Tide,* though not in the same order, follows the same schema.

Wading the Tide is not the unfolding of a single poetic vision, but the manifestation of several personal glimpses, vignettes, as it were, of a most sensitive heart. It was said of Dickens' art that it gained its strength from episodic intensification rather than a painstaking unveiling of a single theme. Doh's poetry gains its strength from scenic intensification - the tendency to exploit to the full, possibilities of any particular scene, event, character, idea, emotion or insight. It can always be argued in a general sense that the thirty-five poems have no center of gravity, no organic unity in the Aristotelian sense, that they are thirty-five different angles of vision from which he expresses his outrage.

In a more analytic sense, each poem is a small world, almost complete in itself. The advantages of such "a God's eye-view" device are legion. A collection of poems so conceived, for instance, may not succeed as a totality, yet intermittently it is bound to achieve the vigour of a masterpiece. Wherein lie the moments of achievement, of less success, it is for the reader to decide. In a poem like T.S. Eliot's "The Waste Land" the poet can be said to have thrown a pebble into a pool from which we watch ripples spread in the form of the movements or sections. In *Wading the Tide,* however, Doh has thrown four pebbles (UPRISING, TRIBUTE, NOSTALGIA, THE OUTCAST) from which we find interlocking ripples (Down Time-Avenue, Bamenda *Chop Fire,* Meeting after So Long, The Taste of Foam, respectively from each section) criss-crossing, overlapping from different angles.

Connoisseurs will be quick to discover that there is no fixed metre, no rhyme scheme and the like. Doh gives a damn. And we cannot blame him for lacking what he never needed in the first place. Here is reason without rhyme. Rhyme, for Doh (the first and last musical notes of the octave!), is an incidental or shall we say accidental adjunct to his craft. We find rhymes occasionally, as

> *Land of prawns*
> *packed full of prawns*
> ...
>
> *learn to swim.*
> *They can't see why other prawns swim*

But these are the exception rather than the rule.

One of the first things to strike you in this rare poetic composition is its simplicity of language and its appropriateness to the subject matter. Doh does not seem to me to be a scholar's, or worse still, a scholarly poet. He is not esoteric. *Wading the Tide* flows from the pen of a poet of the people. To borrow Wordsworth's expression, it is the poetry of a man speaking to other men.

The dominant mood of the collection is one of outrage, gloom and decadence, the vision apocalyptic. He is visibly pained by what he sees, smells, hears and even touches. He is angry, but not so acrimonious as not to be able to communicate meaning. The choice of such epithets as scholarly, coterie and esoteric, invites comparison with his fire-eater compatriot, Bate Besong, popularly called "the Obasinjom Warrior." Doh's indignation is not virulent but controlled and edifying. He does not "shit", or, as Kofi Yankson once said of Ayi Kwei Armah (of *The Beautyful Ones Are Not let Born*) he does not "flatulate through the pen."

The simplicity, however, may be deceptive, for emotional intensity is not incompatible with simplicity of style and subject matter. Doh seems to know more than most other poets of his generation that poetry need not be strange or insipid to be moving.

Besides, the metaphors and imagery are fresh, the simple words unmystical, and have about them a rare sinewy strength, intellectual gravity and a compulsive vitality. Every image reinforces and is absorbed into the poet's mood of unredeemed despair. They have an excitement, eagerness, sincerity, and depth of feeling that stir the emotions.

This is the kind of language which takes us beyond the surface of our own responses by its fresh apprehension and expression of the commonplace, and by the satisfaction it brings to our own inadequate insights and words. In a word, therefore, in *Wading the Tide*, it can be pointed out that Emmanuel Fru Doh has broken much new ground, using very familiar implements.

Linus T. Asong (1994)

Uprising...

Down Time-Avenue

Blessed I am
from that triangle to emerge
the heart of love, peace herself,
the melting pot of all
that nature can award to a limb:
the heat, dryness, and sandy
terrain of the north;
the forest decked with freshness.
and richly foliaged giants;
the waters and humidity of the South, South-West.
and the East; the beautiful greenery of the
undulating grassfields of the North-West.

The beautiful and welcoming smiles
on the faces;
like a pentecostal brood
they are gifted in tongues.
A peace-loving flock,
yes I'm blessed indeed:
the rich game on land and in water
nature's seal of love.

But down Time-Avenue my heart aches:
from afar I hear the muted cries
of a people who know not how to handle a
strange tide as those to direct and protect,
like a purgative, drain the entrails
and leave the triangle hungry;
their deeds the
butcher's hatchet that dissects.

They care less
what our plight is;
at all cost they seek the steering,
even against the wish of passengers
who dread the many ghastly accidents -
social, political and economic -

3

these drivers have barely survived,
thanks to "chez nous."
From yesterday to today,
I wonder in awe, for never before
could I have imagined
a day like today.

The Seasons

Appearance, not ideas, they cheered;
words, not actions, they praised;
hibernated hopes out of mental cocoons
emerged. Faces radiant with smiles
at the arrival of a "messiah,"
the start of a new season.

Appearances now fading
without the materialisation of ideas
their cheers to maintain;
words now confused,
no actions their praises
to preserve. The faces are gloomy,
those smiles gone,
their hopes dethroned by despair.
The times are worse,
the tide of a new season.

Eyes are on the horizon, with
sighs smuggled out that respiration
may survive: disillusionment,
the trademark of the contents of the heart.
On the faces displayed: longing
for the arrival of a genuine messiah
to free my people,
the hopes of a new season.

Kwashiorkor Graveyard

Thou graveyard of my pre-natal chair,
thou preserver of my navel,
gifted in all to make me happy:
fertility, fruitfulness.
Yet today thou art accused -
a kwashiorkor patient - lacking
in vital vitamins: minerals, oil,
agricultural products, foreign exchange.
Treason! It is the tapper who squanders
all the wine and says bad weather
affected the raffia palms; he drinks
the oil and says the kernels
were barren.
Grey heads beginning to lie?
Parents lying to their children?
I fear for tomorrow, for when
awareness shall dawn,
the bad weather shall be purged
and the kernels' barrenness cleansed
or else limbs shall fly.

Njangi House

Representatives my foot.
From North to South
from East to West they
claim to have come - errand boys
and girls. Yet before
they sit, the fruits of
our labour to squander, they
care less our opinions to sample.

They sit with bloated jowls
suffocating in the coated heat
with earphones at ridiculous
angles, state colours from
shoulder to hip like church-wardens.

5

Absent-mindedness in their looks,
siesta time for others,
for what is there to discuss?
only to start and join the others already
clapping.

Some - children - vying for the lens
with lips curled in slovenly smiles
mistaken for the philosophical pose;
heads nodding like fallen lizards, as if
the point struck home, fawning curs.
And then folders are folded,
the end or a session.
RUBBER-STAMPS!

Quite a Deal

Traitors! Demagogues! Bla roads,
bla money, bla high living standards.
But before this midwife takes his turn
on duty, realisation strikes home.
Midwife - sincerely I'm but a killer;
Poverty, starvation, soldiers about me,
coats of mail for I'm frightened
by the idea of death.
Illusions of a guilt-ridden mind:
memories of a dying village - natural
memories of dying children - no drugs,
memories of starving families - no money,
promises all down the drain.
Yet like a colossus I stand
with convoluted jowls
dripping foreign account numbers;
to sell my house and squander
the cash under the rain.

Land of Prawns

Land of prawns
packed full of prawns
limited to their water space,
forbidden to try if they can
learn to swim.
They can't see why other prawns swim;
they hear of student-prawns causing bubbles
in their pool, yet they are not pushed
the cause of bubbles to find out.

Contented these prawns are,
to stay afloat in waters
that quiet they appear
where plankton they can't find.
The prawns sigh, the best
they can for fear of being
flushed out of the waters.
They don't know their brains
are meant for thinking,
their mouths to correct.
Quiet yours prawns appear to be;
no, afraid of the prawn to fish-size grown,
of the prawns brainwashed and transformed
to eliminate prawns trying to produce bubbles.

Land of prawns
it is in the culture of prawns to cause
bubbles in dirty waters; it will
come if not now, soon. Let the prawns
learn to swim and cause bubbles that
all may move well in this water
where prawns bathe and get drunk,
then sleep and cause no bubbles. Calm
the water appears, but the bubbles will rise.

The Bloody Caps

The bloody caps are a shame,
bastardized children of a green
and blue-black parentage.
To help their father, a paramilitary
gang they claim to be, yet they
distort their mother's image

Whenever like dogs they are
unleashed to raid, rape and plunder
citizens in the name of law and order.
A disgrace they are,
effeminated bulls bellowing with
excitement as they spew bullets
at our unarmed fathers, mothers,
sons and daughters. Security!

Security my foot;
let them wait until across frontiers they
are called upon to face their peers
and we shall see how trigger happy
their trigger-happy fingers will be
their answers to citizens in distress:
we're only two at the station,
we can't come; there is no vehicle here,
we can't come; call the police.
Neither nors; wasted taxes.

This is my *Chop-Chair*

For decades a good pupil
of *Alhadji*'s you were,
yet crisis - the wage
of the masses -
ushered by Iscariot and his kind,
legalized barons of multicoloured ills
with bursting coffers alienated,
with profits from our sweat exiled.

8

Alas this hive in chaos.
the queen growing fatter though egg-less
her swollen abdomen a curse,
a storehouse for all and even the
widow's mite. Words, words,
promises, strategies, measures:
the king a toddler doodling with concepts
while his unpatriotic heart
the real solutions harbours.
Woe to the proletariat,
that giant cockroach without feelers
dancing in the dark
to unpatriotic vibrations of demagogic
meaninglessness has ruined us.
Thanks *Alhadji*,
such a will to bequeath posterity.

The Politician Never *Learns*

Only the politician makes the
same mistake twice;
only the politician is the
second fool;
he alone never learns.
He is praised at the dawn of his tenure
and stripped bare as the
years roll by.
Yet, year in year out, he fights
to renew his disgrace;
he is fooling himself,
this second fool.

Lament of the Town-Crier

(For Ntemfac Ofege, Charlie Ndi-Chia and Boh
Herbert)

What hypocritical existence
you prefer, you kings of third
world clans. Shivering at the
truth; persecuting the town-criers
for ringing their bells too loud,
for giving the news too straight
and endangering your sycophantic existence
with vulture-masters of so-called
first-worlds. With them you soar,
devouring the cadavers of your people
whose souls their country's
starving coffers cannot retain
within their shrunken bodies -
journalists of the economic predicament
of their fatherland.

Traitors, to train a town-crier then
control the ringing of his bell;
brainwashing him into a praise-singer
instead of his peoples' eyes, ears, and mouth.
A parrot is caged for telling the truth,
and beaten by un-schooled uniforms - the
vermin of society - hand-picked
to protect their benefactors;
a parrot is no parrot if it cannot report
for fear of the master's rage,
for fear his
resounding beak would be withdrawn.
Helplessly some sit behind powerful bulbs
blaring forth lies from the master's machinery.
When the tide shall turn,
many shall go overboard.

Bamenda *Chop Fire*

Bamenda *chop fire*:
Camouflaged outfit
with guns in war-like readiness
hungry mouths perched on walkie-talkies
microphones gingerly gripped by crooks,
loaded jeeps zooming to and fro
transporting worn-out riot helmets.
In a trance they appear to be,
confused whether they swore
to eliminate or protect citizens
Bamenda *chop fire*.

Bamenda *chop fire*:
Babies, mothers, husbands,
Women: girls, the young, the old,
the very old;
Men: boys, the young, the old,
the very old
even *takumbeng* with displayed greying
groins and sagging breasts,
worn out by maternal callings,
for a curse;
All violated the scorching sun
to say enough is enough,
to the ruins of a
once popular political dream:
Le R E N O U V E A U!
With their guns on the ready
a lone miserable 'copter splashing
away in the sky, raining tear-gas
Bamenda had gone berserk,
enough was enough
Bamenda *chop fire*.

Bamenda *chop fire*:
The soldiers, the tear-gas canisters,
The grenades, amputated limbs
disappeared husbands and sons,

the rape of daughters and mothers
before parents, husbands, children,
brothers and sisters alike;
the whips, drinking of military urine,
bathing in dust in Sunday-white communion
garments, all to break the will of the people.
Like rocks they let the stream of soldiers
have their fill; the provocation,
all to make them fight back that the dreaded
lot be hiroshimaed failed;
congratulations my people for knowing
when to react and when to hold your patience.
The will of the people is supreme,
virtue will always laugh last,
even if "God cannot change the results..."
Bamenda *chop fire*.

Bamenda *chop fire*:
Even though we continue to labour in vain,
dusty roads for the dry season,
muddy gullies for the rainy season,
frequently interrupted power supply,
high water bills,
belated salaries, if any at all,
while alienated leaders fly above our plight;
even though the U.N. with her devil's alternative
may not react until pools of blood begin to flow,
we have made our point.
We are the minority indeed,
but if your bastard mentor could go,
then you will surely go too.
Time is the ultimate judge
and the will of the suffering masses
the path of justice.
Bamenda *chop fire*.

Life on Campus

To every freshman bequeathed
the olive of our forefather's endeavours.
Some with enthusiasm cart around
fiscal stamps, forms, papers to fill;
others defeated already by
grounded rumours of intellectual
torments - a year or two to waste
before degenerating into academic
refugees.
Life on campus.

Life on campus.
with tired buildings
by nature conquered at
our academic dawn:
grass on roof tops, dirt
all around, small-poxed tarmacs,
with taxis hooting in and out
of our undulating wilderness.
Misery!
Life on campus

Life on campus
with two percent pass norms
and a brooding and helpless bunch
of students, driver ants in their
determination and habit of milling
around, uncertain who to meet.
Misery on their faces,
they seek refuge in the cafeteria
waiting to troop in, in September,
or dance to another faculty
for good while their unsure mentors
snarl at them with unfulfilled
political dreams.
Hypocrites!
Life on campus.

Life on campus,
to class or a beauty contest?
Like butterflies they waft along
but some glide, gallop, and slouch,
the results of hopelessness.
And then soldiers!
Killing, raping, looting
chaos - they dared complain,
Life on campus.

And Satan himself,
some politicized academic-Judas,
oversees this inferno.

Shame Africa

Shame Africa
the second fool;
the fool indeed;
after thirty rains,
independence we call it.
After thirty rains when we,
the shackles of dependence
considered shaken off;
after thirty rains when white soldiers raped our villages,
our women, and their politicians
our coffers,
here they come again at the
invitation of bastardized leaders,
leaders without souls, to bask in
opulence - the stolen sweat of
a people. Puppets with strings in
white claws, shamelessly owning to
alienated pupillage.
After thirty rains,
here they come again,
"to protect their nationals,"
they claim, and all
Africa can do is stare;

14

once more Africa ablaze,
once more black blood spewing the streets,
and this blatant invasion
is ignored by the world.

Shame Africa,
that thirty rains after
but for the dreaded elephant,
the Mwalimu, the Bikos and Mandelas,
all else are puppets with chicken hearts,
gamboling curs for leaders.
After draining us with the assistance
of treasonable leaders they kick us
into lines to receive their remains -

"for Africa" they claim.
Let black blood flow,
bur this time let it not stop
until all exploiters are no more.
Like Guinea the rest will toil
but tomorrow we will smile.
Let the blood of traitors
purge this continent if need be,
that Africa may tomorrow be
peopled by patriots.

Negritude At Dusk

Apostle and propagator of *negritude*!
 another fountain of the ink
of black Africa's panegyrics,
of black Africa's pride;
tiger who made me feel my *tigritude*!
Manager of my coloured-brothers and
sisters!
After all this,
the tamas of Africa are muted
and Africa's sexuality rendered impotent.
The beautiful demi-jour of Africa,

the setting of *negritude*, betrayed they
are for *negritude* to retire
into *Europetude*. The ageing tiger
from the forest rains to the city
snow, soiling yourself once more with the
vile contagion of "civilization."
Negritude, son of our soil
abandon thy alienating abode
else be damned a hypocrite,
a double-headed gorgon.
Return into thy tiger skin
and a tiger all through be, that
your words may germinate and
bear fruit, instead of a tiger yesterday,
a bear today.

The Black Queen

It beats my mind,
a white monster, well dressed, polished.
He thinks he is the only man,
but that is a woman on her knees,
just fallen as I can see,
and this monster is still rushing
towards a fallen black woman.
Monster! Do you know she
could be somebody's wife?
Some black son's mother?
Woe to you woman,
he who could face this monster
is behind bars.
The white monster, you got guts? To
attack a helpless woman in the streets?
Where you come from, have
you no respect for age, female age:
From between which thighs you first crept,
from between which thighs you first blinked
at the sun's rays.

16

I look closely at her,
yes, I can see the pain
as she kneels there on the pavement,
clutching to her bag and glasses
with the white monster on the attack.
Barbarian!
In spite of the pain,
I see the stoic on her knees
and my heart is heavy. White
monster, is that how you treat women?
I know it is because it is day and other
monsters with bared fangs are ready to help.
Were it dark, a boy, a kaffir,
would have shown you what it means
to have a penis between
black instead of scalded thighs.

What did you do to her?
If you celled her have you raped her
to discover that unique taste?
If you killed her have you eaten her?
Just part of you I know,
but the tide will turn.

Who Do They Think They Are Fooling

Who do they think they are
fooling? To come here and
ask us to plant tea, cotton
banana, coffee, and rubber,
for their industries,
who do they think they are fooling?

Who do they think they are fooling?
And then they reduce buying prices and
our farmers are frustrated.
They rush in with financial aid and
loans on condition that we plant more
tea, cotton, banana, coffee and rubber.
Who do they think they are fooling?

Who do they think they are fooling?
They hang metres and we pay for the
metres and our water;
they hang metres and we pay for the
metres and power generated by our streams.
Who do they think they are fooling?

Tribute...

The *Maquisards*

Born in chaos, baptized
in chaos, schooled in chaos,
have lived in chaos.
People did you know them?
Our brothers, our fathers, our husbands,
our sisters, our mothers, our wives,
those who could
look into tomorrow - and knew
the trend of things,
tradition was being abused - to see
for the good of all.

Murderers! They were presented
as such, people who just killed
women and children without cause,
but now we know the truth.
Too many things were going wrong
so they fought against them
to set things right and let
our own be our own.
With strange reasons they were
arraigned and shot in various home-towns
like petty criminals and he, God's prelate,
adopted by the Vatican. But today,
we the owners are begging from pilferers,
those they fought to hold at bay.
They were fired in their home-towns,
accused of treason and branded *maquisards,*
but today we know they were not *maquisards,*
terrorists, but genuine patriots.
O woe that can't be erased,
like hens and chicks frightened of
the hawk, we lived, we lived and live
unable to vocalize,
unable to plan for our future.
No, I say it is not a hawk
but a mere cock soaring above
with the lust for dissenter elimination.

Our martyrs were correct
they had the eyes to see but we committed
suicide directing the uninvited
legionnaire- - "protector" to his camp.
I look over the horizon, the setting sun
is blazing red, tortured
to death by darkness, yet tomorrow
if not the same son, another daughter
of ours shall rise. This time
our view has changed. We shall
clap at the bang... bang!
I fear what I see at the top of Fako,
of Kilimanjaro,
and unless the God of goodness
 intervenes, these volcanoes,
shall vent their steam and the
lava shall flow.

The Poet-Soldier
(For Major General Mamman Vatsa)

The pen and the gun
eternal opposites they be;
the one deceptively calm
the other deadly it looks
yet the more deadly is calmness.

Bring not the two together
for the treacherous inferiority complex
of the latter shall choke the
Life-force out of the former
like the breath from his lungs - Okigbo.

Then Mamman,
the two all in one
a self at war with itself.
the intellect and the beast,
the beast in him won and his brains
like his predecessor's splattered
at a bang.

22

Divorce such marriages
let the pen reign, guide and teach
but contaminate no more those
fingers that grip the noblest master
with the touch of a brutish brainless metal.
For too long I have mourned.
add not another to the list
and make idle brains honoured
for the transition of men of substance.

More into the secret cult delve
that only the initiated may decipher
thy tongue and the gun will be lost.
And while the young and innocent
shall learn the word, no more brains
shall paint the dark walls of dungeons
or plant poetic genius on lawns.

The Light That Never Shone
(For Bernardine Neh Doh)

Generosity incarnate,
gentleness personified,
generous and gentle Bernardine
what a pain oh sun, to set before
rising? Our hopes were crushed
out of us and like the juice from
an orange fruit
our hopes flowed from our eyes.

Let not my silence deceive that late
heart of yours, let not the fact that
the priest fails to announce
"for Bernardine, may her soul
rest in peace," turn thy love into
hurt. Dear little one,
I was just a kid yet to learn
the needs of those in the eternal realm

when death's blow struck and my
integrity, like the temple at
Christ's death, crumbled.

Now I begin to see a ray of hope,
more than a decade since the start
of your journey into eternity.
Be then my guide, my mentor
along the thorny way to the gold mine
that when my sun shall set
I may feel that gentle hand once
more in mine
leading me to my reward.

Just After Nine Rains

O gentle sister
genius to have been, gentleness
and love, generosity personified,
flushed from this hole of woe just
after nine rains. Yes this hole of woe,
hence dilemma in flesh I am for I know
not whether to squeeze dry my flooded
eyeballs for tears - the husband of pain –
since I cannot see your gentle face
and listen to your friendly voice any
longer, or to hold back the husband of
pain from divorce with my eyeballs,
and jubilate instead that you are
free from this cauldron
cooking of malice.

Farewell terrestrial queen of peace,
of love and generosity,
but let not the comfort of the heavenly
abode block your throat against
our libation, thy eardrums to our pleas
for when the storm shall rise and the
bubbles from this boiling cauldron

threaten to swallow us,
wine on your lonely residence we shall
pour and your name invoke
that celestial help may reach us.

Hence I won't sadden your stay with
my tears. Prepare therefore a room
in our father's mansion for our
impending homecoming.
Meanwhile, be our guide and guard
and so strengthen the gates to our
home from those who wish us not well.

To A Queen At Dusk
(For Mrs. Menyoli née Laura Ewenye Nganda)

Queen of the mountain
pearl of the shore
gem among stones
diamond between a hog's trotters -
Ewenye - is it true you are no more?
To stride this earth
whetting men's appetite
whetting children's admiration
with your beauty
with your generosity,
consoling the tormented with that
radiant smile, only to set
just like that...

What a commodity
for life and death to batter with!
Where were you all when the light
in Nganda's lantern was being put out?
What else can survive this queen
of the coast if not woe?
What else can survive this family-
corner-stone if not bitterness?

Is it true there is *la'mbor*,[1]
and our ancestors welcome you
with your meagre thirty-nine?

If you must leave us behind,
then rest dear sister,
but let your light lead us on
that tomorrow - as they say -
we may meet to part no more,
and by your celestial fireside at dusk,
remember,
you shall tell us the truth
of your slim and beautiful thirty-nine.

Kamah

You, you grandmother - vague!
Eyes of four saw you sitting by
a bag of groundnuts mixed with
the paste of grassland pears which
the toiling engines down the
slope had made ready prematurely,
as you rolled down to see your children
at the coast.

Tall, slim, friendly face; giving me
groundnuts. I did not know then, that
you were the source of my source.
Now you are beyond the clouds.
From Marcus I can tell what the
wife was like - Kamah!

---

[1]In lamnso', a language spoken by the Kumbo people of the North West Province of Cameroon, *La'mbor* can be translated to mean heaven.

And They Killed Che-Ngwa Ghandi

At best a smile
and a soft spoken word of greeting
was all he could give to friends
and foe alike.

Politics was not his game
but church-going.
Then suddenly his office is
raided - the State of Emergency -
an enemy had named Ghandi one of
the "vandals." But this is a lie
and she the whore knew
that she had lied.

Without questions, like a common
criminal, Ghandi was whisked
off in handcuffs up the station
hill to discuss with blood-thirsty
curs who know no language but
the inflicting of pain.
We hear they hung him upside down
we hear they beat him upside down
we hear with strange instruments they tore
out his toe-nails with chunks of flesh
to make him confess a lie.
"I did not do it." Ghandi wept.
We hear they beat the soles of his feet
we hear they urinated on his wounds
we hear they refused him medical attention
when for days his entrails had not moved.
Begging relatives were insulted
begging colleagues slighted
and when it was all late they
dumped him in their garbage heap
of a hospital;
and Ghandi died.

We hear it was his brother
they wanted, but anyone
from the family could do
to pacify the whims of the powers
that be; the power whose sister's
shack they claimed Ghandi had stoned.

Wherever they may be
whoever they may be
the perpetrators of such viciousness
the conceivers of such wickedness,
If indeed there is a God, and I know
there is, may His curse alight on
their children's children
until the end of the generation of
Ghandi's offspring.

The Quest
(For Njoh Chrysantus)

Academic refugees we were –
escaping from knowledge truncation
escaping from academic malnutrition
- for years in exile
rescued by a neighbouring complex.

The hunger, the strifes, the risky trips
to and fro we withstood; every wrinkle,
though green in years, a proof of
academic maturity.
O sower, alas, at the threshold
of the harvesting season,
to return with your harvest
that dependants may breathe a
sigh of relief and posterity salvaged
with a balanced diet, when BANG!
triggered by a worthless soul,
dirt, a vermin, and down
crashed a colossus.

Santos, are all the years of toiling
and hope, all the prints come to this?
Why should Gentleness, Generosity,
Encouragement, and Virtue die,
and Vice left to reign?
What is the world come to,
for a few grains?

And yet we argued
our last services to you,
for some their only, to perform,
while your fatherland rejected you,
and so are we all, for Santos
had collected his repatriation mite.

Ah vultures! Bur friends,
with all due respects,
disregarding our hopeless embassy,
joined his umbilical cord again to his navel
and not abandoned like a worthless
war casualty. Hypocrites!

Santos your mysterious hour came;
mine, ours, will come.
The truth, you alone can and will tell;
rest let them live for ever.

The Amazon
(To Ita at the end)

Those early years,
then suddenly, within the greenery of
marriage I left. Calmly and
quietly as ever you waited. Then
the moments of trial: pain, tears,
fears, threats, uncertainty.
As finely as the universe you stood
your ground waiting for Jason.

Here I come, back to you, not
without the fleece. It is more
your victory for I cannot fight
the battle you've fought.

Bamenda

Bamenda, when for the first
time I came, up at the station
I stood and looked:
beautiful by day.
Down in the valley
surrounded by the hills, you looked
like a lake - a lake
of shimmering silver.

Bamenda, for the second
time I came, night had fallen.
I heard the insects shrieking,
the cold up at station;
it was refreshing.
Once more down town I looked:
you glittered, like a valley
bedded by gold.

Bamenda, my lake of zinc by day,
the golden valley by night,
I wait for the time when I will
my last visit to you make,
never to leave you again
but to become part of
you, like Marcus and Martha.

Where I Do Not Belong
(For Professor Moses Fon Asanji)

Meant to be a citadel of
learning but Luciferian whims
to a circus have turned it.
Mentors and their apprentices,
moving academic buffoons:
apathy transformed and want of incentive.

Research is near absent as even the
brain-house for books is kwashiorkor--
stricken, victimized by volume malnutrition;
that which is there, an insult to the idea
with mainly grey volumes.
Infrastructure a joke, yet the most
distinguished demons of this state-hell
commandeered by reedy voice Beelzebub,
graduands they are from this
Sahara of learning - Bambili.

This bazaar,
with academics toyed with
and certificates ridiculously
ranked as francophonie scallywags
transform hard-earned robes
into a circus of harlequins all;
ah, this francophonie buffoonery
with scholastic barometers.

In come the Israelitic heir to pharaoh's
throne from this academic Egypt to free us
after decades of near meaninglessness:
repainted rooms, functioning toilets,
humanism. Yet the way to the promised
land appears away Moses.
But you took the toddling step - the
most important - joining us in this quagmire,
using mud and straw to produce bricks for
tomorrow.

31

Alas with those publications from our
purgatory, academic prince, to
politically-titled professors
without names on shelves you must stoop
to conquer and get us passage
into Ekele-Heaven standards.
You took the first step that some day
this desert an academic meadow may become
for our offspring to graze on in an
academic utopia where we all belong.

Nostalgia...

Meeting After So Long

Gentle, calm and composed,
youthfulness notwithstanding.
I feared to tarnish her radiant
innocence and so I controlled
my wagging tongue and said nothing.
Today, after so many years
have rolled by, she still is in control:
gentle, calm and composed.
But now she talks, and talks big.
She laughs, prattles, teases, and enjoys
her jokes.
But she tells me "Sorry it can't be now,
how I wish we met the last time I was home;
now I'm bound by a promise - sigh - I
won't want to break it.

You are nice, handsome and a
wonderful company. Without my promise
nothing would stop me from yielding."

"I'll wait; I won't push you."

"Wait... wait ... If anything goes wrong ..."

a peck on her left cheek, my reward.

Parting Ways

By some great force it was,
that we converged, all three, at this
uncle, grand uncle, relative's.
And like labourers we worked.
toiled, cleaning the milk-white tiles,
sweeping the thickly rugged floor
with broomsticks, the offspring
of palm-kernel plants; vacuum-cleaning
the thickly carpeted rooms,
vimming the toilet bowls and
wash-hand basins, washing dishes
after dishes after heavily peopled
meals and banquets, washing car after car:
and insults, my reward.

But more important was the company
I met: true brothers but better friends
they were. We ate, drank, slept, lived
and grew up together.
A bond emerged between us
that nothing seemed strong enough
ever to break. But time,
time is stronger than any force
and sharper than any edge,
for it would humble and slice
through the toughest.
With time we went our different ways -
I the condemned - while the rest hoped
for a better tomorrow from where we had
all toiled. With time, that love, that
care, that concern for one another,
seemed to have gone,
while memories flower the garden of my
thoughts. All that which is between
us today is mechanical,
or so, to me, it seems.

Gone With The Seventies

They used to be nice
and understanding
not rude and uncompromising

they used to be modest
and faithful to their vows of poverty
not 'vagant and steeped in opulence

they prayed for the love of prayers
not because people were watching
they prayed as a way of life and not a duty

they zoomed from out-station
to out-station
and would not only city-preachers be

they loved their flock like
their very selves
and would not take without having given

they used to be apostles from
God's earth and not
from Bafut, Mankon, or Bali

at worst, from the public's view
all else they kept and lived indeed
as shepherds of His flock.

they considered themselves
servants of the house
and not masters of the lodge

even in death their humility reigned supreme
the last of the missionaries,
gone with the seventies.

This Maze

It was day
and then night came,
there was light but
it was flooded by darkness;
that is what I saw
there is only one route to
this maze - birth -
and only one way out, death.

What a maze, bumping
into one another, insulting the one
praising the other,
sycophants; present in this maze:
distrust, deceit; a total contravention
of the ten commandments - Pandemonium!

Somewhere at the top corner of out maze
I saw a small hole, through which
a thin ray of light seeped in.
A few were beginning to find their way
but others shaded their eyes
with their hands and staggered along.

The Abyss Of The Past

My eyes turn within,
they span the years long gone
the pleasures float freshly to my heart,
the sorrows surface from the deep,
my eyes turn into a pool,
the joys of pleasure and sorrow.
Life is such a span, of pain
and pleasure, vice and virtue,
decorating the tide of time and events.
We forget them, but some day a simple sound
will brighten the dark alley of the past, your

heart will be heavy, heavy like mine now,
with a sigh I returned,
yes returned to the present.

Dilemma Children

Native soil, woe to you.
Across thy cool dark bowels
I crawled as a child, playing
with the undulations and
contents of your entrails.
I was happy as a child, age saved me from
recognizing the maliciousness of mankind,
his hypocrisy. Whose people were we
then? Then came scalded-flesh to call us his,
to civilize us he said. Marauder!

Today, that gentle rhythm,
of early morning rising,
the heating of last night's fufu and
bitter-leaf, eating, going to farm,
returning at dusk, heating water,
bathing, roasting maize and boiling
groundnuts; the telling of tales
for them to get done, eating and going
 to bed, is all gone.

The calmness of life is gone,
gone is the talking drum, gone are
those happy voices in the
African twilight as men and women
boys and girls danced to the rhythm of
«barbaric» instruments, ha! ha!
the one teaching, the other learning the
secrets of mother Africa. In place
of calmness has come deadly sounds.
Even our darkness is no longer for dancing
and rejoicing but a den for malicious
events: killing, stealing, trademarks

of the already debauched tradition:
CIVILIZATION!
In this camouflage, a chicken
has become our *fon* from across big

waters. Our ace dogs are now his,
and they defend the pigs instead,
while legalised pilferers are left to
pilfer our belongings and even our souls
in the name of security. In this light
I thirst for barbarity, the reign of
honesty, oneness, happiness and togetherness
- no Swiss banks and foreign banks
to pollute weak minds and through them
siphon our well.
Barbarity or civilization, which way are we?

Rain Clouds

That face of the earth,
the sky, bright and radiant,
then anger rises, the cloud
darkens and the thunder
rumbles and, like the
locomotive engine, gives steam
to the thick black clouds.

Gently this train glides out
of its station, heading, for
the onlooker, to an unknown
destination. But the frown on
that face is unmistaken as
the rain clouds like wrinkles converge.
Unable to accommodate it any more,
the steam is let loose and
the tears flow freely
flooding away the wrinkles from
the face of the earth.

The Outcast...

The Taste of Foam

Foamy eyes, foamy throats
s-s-s-s-s-s-e-e- u - u- p!
the long seep from a foam-crowned mug
satisfying!
Illusory satisfaction amidst vultures
soaring in the sky, in search of
carrions - victims for criticizing the
king of decay.
Is the world just foams all the time,
or is it just this dungeon?
Farmers who care less about the nature
of their harvest in so far as there's foam?
Afraid of the vultures in the sky,
they pretend not to smell the decay
and shamelessly, those with eyes and voices
bury their brains in foam all year round.
Posterity will always question so
put down those foamy thrones and be
Cabrals and Fanons - map out a better day
for posterity.

Samson And Delilah

When towards the colossal
one strives, none notices the travails;
but how all long the colossus to bring down.

How we feed fat on rumours,
how we enjoy slander,
listening to and spreading and with
the demonic painting brush of
the infernal tempter,
polish the colours to suit our
envious whims
all in a bid to crush this colossus.

And in comes Delilah,
Samsonizing in vain;
this puppet of the conspirators.
And coated stories

she churned with that reptilian tongue
to suit the taste of the envious,
and now their chance to tell and tell.
How she strew the streets with
slander and defamation, all
in a bid Samson's thoraxes cage to crack
and so soil his integrity
while giving herself undeserved fame,
while usurping another's crown.

And the verbal strokes of her
tongue her type enjoyed and multiplied.
But nothing is like the conscience,
the sole judge with all the facts.
Let the tongues wag, their greedy
slanderous appetite to satiate, after all
what is the wind to the sun's rays?

Let them say...

Fear The White Man's Country

Fear the white man's country,
some people go there and come back well
some people go there and come back sick
Fear the white man's country.

Fear the white man's country,
some people go there and come back home
some people go there and are heard of no more
Fear the white man's country.

But Blood, they say,
is thicker than water.

44

Like a viper
he lay as he grew,
calm and quiet but
a truant occasionally
like every other child.
But his notoriety he
was never to abandon,
age notwithstanding.
Then his sojourn
in the white man's land
and when he came back
to us he was a whitewashed wall.

Unlike those before him
who returned and had not
forgotten our tongue,
he had forgotten our tongue
he had forgotten those he left behind.
Some said it was the white man's food
some said it was too much of the white man's book
some said it was the white man's weather
the very cold winter and then the warm summer.

They say winter turns your brain into stone
only for summer to come and thaw it into mud;
this confuses some we hear
and turns some into black-white men we hear
but the truth we feared:
people must have sent him
strange stories about home:
his mother, his brothers, his sisters.

Unlike the white man,
after eating all his food
after reading all his book
after sleeping with their women
after summer, fall, winter and spring,
when after all the years he returned
he cared less to find out the truth;
he had condemned us, even
from the white man's land.

And when at last he came,
even the white man does not know
how to speak like a white man;
he spoke *spspspspspsp* as if
he could not open his mouth.
He sat in a kind of white man's
parlour like a god, waiting
for us to come from far and wide
to visit this black-white man.

Unlike those who had returned
before him, he was not happy
to rush and see for himself
those he had left behind for years.
Some thought he wanted to keep
his winter-coats all to himself;
some thought he wanted to use all
the white man's things he had brought alone;
people clapped their hands and said o-oh!

To him, that saying is obsolete,
his blood is lighter than water.
He says he knows nobody, only
his mother, not even the carrier
of shit who gave him birth. He denied
him and thus crushed his heart.
But it was the shit-money
that lay the foundations of
his white man's life,
it was the shit money that
cured his big man's fainting fits.
He says to hell with *country-fashion*
he calls it meaningless superstition.
He cares about nothing, about nobody.
He lives alone, all alone,
like a detainee held incommunicado.
A few people get to know him
tolerate him for a while
and then they are gone.
He claims he needs nobody,
he listens to nobody;

he has no respect from anybody
thanks to the white man's country.

Fear the white man's country,
some people go there and come back well
some people go there and come back sick
Fear the white man's country.

Fear the white man's country,
some people go there and come back home
some people go there and are heard of no more
Fear the white man's country.